Little Bear's
Shapes

Little Bear's Shapes

JANE HISSEY

HUTCHINSON

London Sydney Auckland Johannesburg

square   circle   triangle   rectangle   star   semi-circle

square

square flag

cube   sphere   pyramid   cone   cuboid   cylinder

The toys are cutting out square windows.

square   circle   triangle   rectangle   star   semi-circle

circle

blue circle

Bruno's wooden hoop is a circle.

square   circle   **triangle**   rectangle   star   semi-circle

triangle

red triangle

Little Bear's dragon mask has triangles for teeth.

square   circle   triangle   rectangle   star   semi-circle

rectangle

See-through rectangle

cube   sphere   pyramid   cone   cuboid   cylinder

The bears are all holding paper rectangles.

square   circle   triangle   rectangle   **star**   semi-circle

star

paper star

cube   sphere   pyramid   cone   cuboid   cylinder

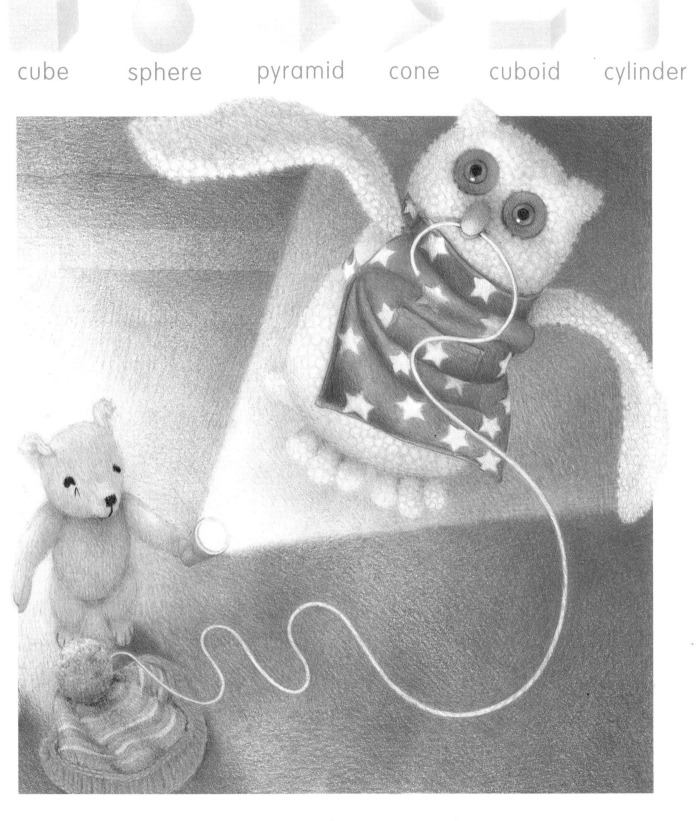

Hoot has stars on her apron.

square   circle   triangle   rectangle   star   semi-circle

semi-circle

biscuit semi-circles

Bramwell is pointing to a yellow semi-circle.

These are all two-dimensional –
2-D – shapes. They are flat.

These are all three-dimensional –
3-D – shapes. They are not flat.

square   circle   triangle   rectangle   star   semi-circle

cube

wooden cubes

cube   sphere   pyramid   cone   cuboid   cylinder

Ruff's birthday cake is a cube.

sphere

glass sphere

cube   sphere   pyramid   cone   cuboid   cylinder

The ball the toys have found is a sphere.

square   circle   triangle   rectangle   star   semi-circle

pyramid

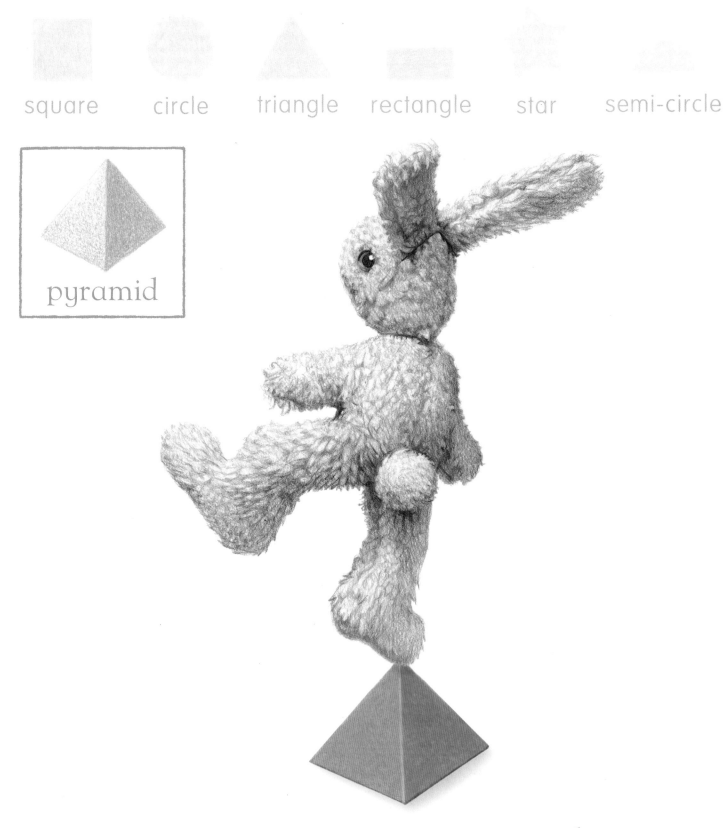

green pyramid

cube   sphere   **pyramid**   cone   cuboid   cylinder

Camel is galloping past some pyramids.

square   circle   triangle   rectangle   star   semi-circle

cone

ice-cream cones

cube   sphere   pyramid   **cone**   cuboid   cylinder

Little Bear and Ruff have cone-shaped hats.

cuboid

cuboid suitcase

Sarah Elizabeth's sewing box is a cuboid.

square circle triangle rectangle star semi-circle

cylinder

wooden cylinder

cube   sphere   pyramid   cone   cuboid   cylinder

Bramwell's rolling pin is a cylinder.

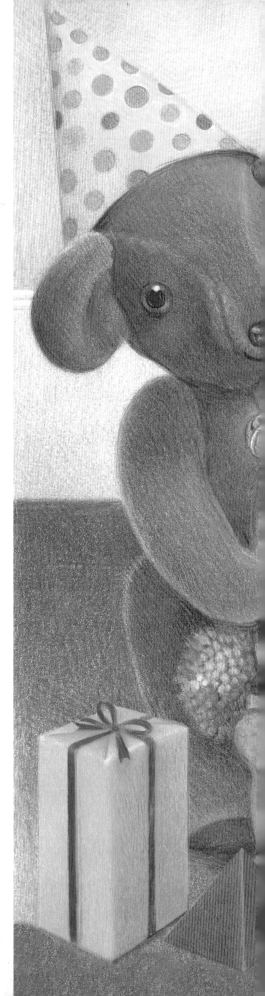

How many shapes
can you find?

For Susan and John

LITTLE BEAR'S SHAPES

A HUTCHINSON BOOK 0 09 188485 3

Published in Great Britain by Hutchinson,
an imprint of Random House Children's Books

This edition published 2003

1 3 5 7 9 10 8 6 4 2

RANDOM HOUSE CHILDREN'S BOOKS
61–63 Uxbridge Road, London W5 5SA
A division of The Random House Group Ltd

RANDOM HOUSE AUSTRALIA (PTY) LTD
20 Alfred Street, Milsons Point, Sydney,
New South Wales 2061, Australia

RANDOM HOUSE NEW ZEALAND LTD
18 Poland Road, Glenfield, Auckland 10, New Zealand

RANDOM HOUSE (PTY) LTD
Endulini, 5A Jubilee Road, Parktown 2193, South Africa

THE RANDOM HOUSE GROUP Limited Reg. No. 954009
www.kidsatrandomhouse.co.uk

A CIP catalogue record for this book is available from the British Library.

Printed in Singapore